11-23

TEACHING THE CATHOLIC CATECHISM

JOSEF GOLDBRUNNER

TEACHING THE
CATHOLIC CATECHISM

with the Religion Workbook

VOLUME II

THE CHURCH AND THE SACRAMENTS

HERDER AND HERDER

This English translation by Bernard Adkins is based on the third German edition of

"Katechismusunterricht mit dem Werkheft,

zweiter Teil, Von der Kirche und den Sakramenten"

published by Kösel, München, 1958

Third impression published 1961 by

Herder and Herder, Inc.,

7 West 46th Street, New York 36, New York

Spanish edition: Editorial Herder, Barcelona

Nihil Obstat: Joannes M. T. Barton, S. T. D., L. S. S.

Censor Deputatus.

Imprimatur: Georgius L. Craven. Vic. Gen., Epus.

Sebastopolis. Westmonasterii, die 25a Mensis Augusti 1959.

The Nihil Obstat and Imprimatur are a declaration that a book or pamphlet is considered to be free from doctrinal or moral error. It is not implied that those who have granted the Nihil Obstat and Imprimatur agree with the contents, opinions or statements expressed.

Made and printed by Herder Druck, Freiburg, West Germany

CONTENTS

FOREWORD

Although the Catechism itself is all-inclusive, the religion lesson generally is not. Depending on the time available or the capacity of the children, the teacher usually chooses only a portion of the material and limits himself to the more important aspects of it.

The three volumes of this commentary, each of which deals with a section of the Catechism, make use of this "art of limitation", and attempt, according to the requirements of each lesson, to emphasize only the central teaching of the various chapters of the Catechism. For that reason, from the majority of Catechism lessons only one religious instruction has been outlined in a form which admits of an *oral* and *visual* development.

The oral part, following the same sequence throughout (AIM, PREPARATION, PRESENTATION, EXPLANATION, APPLICATION), contains the ideas being set forth in the instruction, and provides all the necessary factual information. The AIM indicates the purpose of the instruction: what it is striving devoutly to achieve. The PREPARATION, by concrete examples taken directly from everyday life, seeks to arouse the attention and to focus it on the aim of the instruction. The PRESENTATION exposes to the eyes the mind – and often to the eyes of the body as well – what is to be reflected upon by the students. In the EXPLANATION some new truth or aspect of truth is arrived at by the class either through its own efforts or by means of the teacher's observations. The APPLICATION attempts to construct a bridge back again to the world of everyday life. Situations are chosen from the realm of ordinary, commonplace events to which the newly acquired knowledge is applied. From a purely religious point of view, the application should not be regarded as the climax of the instruction. The high point of the lesson is to be found in the presentation or explanation.

It follows, then, that the sacred nature of the instruction is not infringed upon when use is made of discussions and debates, or even occasionally of short one-act plays: by these means religion is placed in its natural background and does not become isolated from daily life. Class discussions and more especially debates have, of course, to be practised by the students, for only gradually will they venture to offer an opinion; but as confidence increases the students will be brought quite freely and readily to contribute to the enrichment of the lesson.

A teacher with a flair for dramatic work will be amazed at how fruitful for catechetical instruction the religious play can be. For example, the play, *Getting Up,* on page 64, may prove to be an excellent way of practising or revising the morning prayers. As the children grow less and less constrained, they will take great delight in dramatizing these subjects.

The oral instruction and blackboard summary are complementary. The summary recalls at a glance the aim and development of the instruction. The suggested drawings (so easy to copy that little class time need be devoted to them) are the fruit of long experience. It is not beyond the power of any child to reproduce them. Experience has also shown that children display ingenious flights of fancy in the decoration of these drawings in their workbooks. If the teacher himself has doubts about his ability to sketch these drawings, a little practice outside the classroom will bring considerable facility. But even if the children do not copy the drawings, their presence on the blackboard will contribute to the lesson.

Directions for coloring: water=blue; stones=white; wood=brown; symbols for God and the supernatural life=yellow; the Holy Spirit and love=red; the crosses to represent Christians=green.

Five minutes at the end of each lesson should suffice for the children to copy the blackboard summary into a scrapbook; at home they can then transfer it to their workbooks.

The Catechism itself is used in preparing the lesson, during the lesson for reference, and finally for revision. Homework may consist of reading the Catechism lesson and answering the questions posed under the heading, CONSIDER. This reading of the text helps to strengthen and to complete the instruction given in class, while serving as a useful basis for review.

Blackboard summary, Catechism, workbook: with continued use, these three will be found to combine effortlessly together.

45. JESUS CHRIST BEGAN TO LAY THE FOUNDATION OF HIS CHURCH DURING HIS PUBLIC LIFE

AIM. The foundation of the Church, as pre-eminently the work of Christ, and that from the beginning a threefold division in the Church was to be seen.

PREPARATION. The first lesson introduces the theme of the course – the Church and her sacraments.

From the very beginning the twofold meaning of the word "Church" must be made quite clear: as the house of God (=the church building); and as the community of believers, the people of God.

Whenever we now speak of the Church we mean the people of God.

PRESENTATION. Three gospel scenes are portrayed: 1. How Christ gathered his disciples about him. 2. How he chose the apostles from among them. 3. How he chose Simon Peter to be the rock of the Church.

EXPLANATION. By means of the blackboard summary. From the Christus-symbol three rays are drawn; they represent the three actions of Christ described above. Green crosses stand for the disciples, that is the believers, who are now called Christians. The shepherds' croziers represent the Apostles (= those sent), and the key stands for Peter (= the Rock). Underneath are written the names by which they are known today. Apostle = Bishop, Peter = Pope.

Thus the foundations of the Church were laid. A bracket joins all three together as the people of God called together from among all the nations of the earth. The gradual building up of the blackboard summary itself serves as an effective explanation.

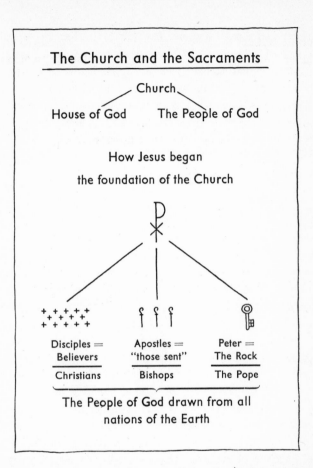

The Church and the Sacraments

Church

House of God   The People of God

How Jesus began

the foundation of the Church

Disciples = Believers	Apostles = "those sent"	Peter = The Rock
Christians	Bishops	The Pope

The People of God drawn from all
nations of the Earth

APPLICATION. Has much time passed since the Church was founded? Yes and No. How many generations have passed since Christ died? If we assume one generation to last thirty years we should get 65 generations. The passage from parents to children has occured sixty-five times. But that isn't a lot. The apostles of the first generation of Christians are really quite close to us. PLAY. Each child acts the part of a representative of one of the great nations of the earth. As Catholic Christians they are making a pilgrimage to Rome where they meet on the great square before St. Peter's. They tell each other about the people they come from. (What the children have learnt from geography, etc.).

46. BY HIS DEATH JESUS CHRIST WON LIFE FOR HIS CHURCH

AIM. The meaning of Christ's death for the people of God. The price payed for the future life in God's Kingdom.

The basic theme of this instruction is, therefore, the *commercium divinum* at the throne of grace, diagrammatically portrayed by the scales.

PREPARATION. Christ not only collected together and taught the new People of God. More important, he raised them up to a new life. He unlocked the source of a new life (grace-life) for God's people. That cost him a very high price.

PRESENTATION. a. The scales help us to understand what happened. Jesus placed the purchase price, that is, his body and blood, on one side of the scales. They are the sacrificial gifts given for our Redemption; for the grace-life for God's People.

b. What did God the Father give in return? What did he lay on the other side of the scales? He gave the key of heaven.

c. With this key Christ opened the sources out of which now flows grace-life upon his Church: the Sacraments.

d. Since then the Church has lived upon this source of grace-life. For this reason Christ said to Peter "I will give thee the key of

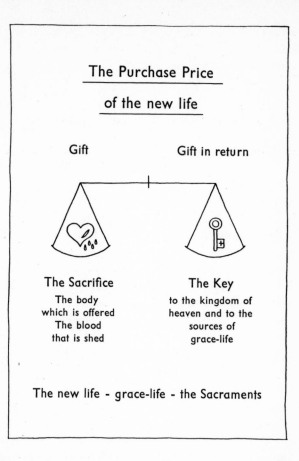

The Purchase Price

of the new life

Gift   **Gift in return**

The Sacrifice   **The Key**
The body   to the kingdom of
which is offered   heaven and to the
The blood   sources of
that is shed   grace-life

The new life - grace-life - the Sacraments

the kingdom of heaven". Peter passed it on to his successor, the Pope. The practise has continued down to our own time. For this reason the keys of the kingdom have always featured in the papal coat of arms.

APPLICATION. We have the key to the waters of the new life which we call grace-life. The sources of the water from which we drink are the sacraments.

47. AFTER HIS RESURRECTION JESUS COMPLETED THE FOUNDING OF HIS CHURCH

AIM. Through the sending of the Holy Spirit, the Church recieves life just as the body of Adam was given life by the spirit breathed into it.

PREPARATION. Does the Church lack anything? Is she not like the body of Adam on the day of his creation, before the disease of sin had broken out? At Pentecost there took place a new creation. That of the Church.

PRESENTATION. At Pentecost the Apostles waited in the Cenacle for the coming of the Holy Ghost. In Peter, the Apostles and the assembled Faithful the Church became visible.

EXPLANATION. Peter, the apostles and the disciples now appear for the first time as the people of God. Who had brought that about? Comparison: The body of Adam and the breathing in of life on the day of creation. In the same way the people of God is a body in which the Holy Spirit dwells – as it were, its soul.

Thus at Pentecost the founding of the Church was completed and the Church began to live.

APPLICATION. Throughout the centuries the Church has lived through this mysterious power of the Holy Spirit. In all dangers and persecutions her mysterious life-power has proved itself, showing thus visibly the meaning of the sending of the Holy Spirit. There is no foundation or institution on earth to be compared with the Church.

Jesus Christ completed

the foundation of the Church

Body ⟷ Soul

People of God ⟷ Holy Spirit

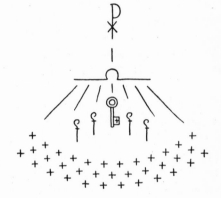

The Holy Spirit is the soul of the Church

DISCUSSION. Compare the foundation of a business, a firm, a State, their difficulties and duration. What connection with the Church had the following: Nero, Helena, Constantine, Athanasius (o similar well-known figures)?

48. THE CHURCH IS THE MYSTICAL BODY OF CHRIST

AIM. The doctrine of the reality of the Mystical Body of Christ is so difficult that we deal here with only one aspect of it, namely the external comparison with a body whose members are bound to each other.

PREPARATION. The body and soul of the Church as distinguished in the preceding instruction. The body of the Church (= the people of God), can be compared with a human body.

PRESENTATION. A picture of Christ on the cross in the romanesque style, i.e., dressed in royal robes, the arms outstretched. Considering the external form, one is reminded of the ground plan of a church with transept. (There are churches in the Tyrol with the sanctuary, as the inclined head of Christ, built at an angle to the nave.)

EXPLANATION. On the ground plan of a church the head and the members are distinguished. In the sanctuary there stands the altar. It represents Christ the head of God's people: in the nave the pillars are drawn in = the apostles as pillars of God's people; then the Saints (for example at the side altar) – and then the people of God. Pope, bishops, and believers (green crosses for the believers). The sole point of this explanation is the comparison of the ground plan with Christ on the cross.

APPLICATION. From this comparison we learn that all members of the Church belong together and are united together, each with the others and with the head. As our relationship to Christ is more often emphasized let the emphasis here be in particular upon "Christian brotherly love".

PLAY. An example of Christian brotherly love. A motor accident. A school friend lies in the street seriously wounded. The adults

The Church

is the Mystical Body of Christ

Body = Head and members

Christ is the head
We are the members
Pillars = Apostles

Our task: Christian brotherly love

have sent for a doctor and the police. You kneel beside him and say short prayers with him.

DISCUSSION. How ought Christian brotherly love to show itself: in the home, on the sportsfield, on the buses, in shops, among workers in a factory, between employer and employed, in industry?

49. THE HOLY CONSTITUTION OF THE CHURCH

AIM. A glance at the hierarchical order of God's people. It is the same which Christ made at the beginning.

PREPARATION. Look back to Lesson 45 to see how Christ began with the Church. The threefold division into disciples – apostles – Peter.

PRESENTATION AND EXPLANATION. The Pope's coat of arms in St. Peter's, Rome: the key of heaven in the succession of St. Peter (264 Popes), the triple tiara, its weight, external and internal. St. Peter's Square and St. Peter's Basilica as the meeting place of all nations: the Pope rules over the Universal Church.

The Universal Church is divided into small sections, called dioceses. Each is cared for by a bishop (approximately 1000 dioceses and bishops). The dioceses are divided into parishes. (Give the number of parishes in your diocese.) Each parish is cared for by the parish priest sent by the bishop. The parish priest is helped by assistants (a crossed stole as the symbol for a priest).

The believers – also called the laity – when gathered before the altar of their parish church together with the priest, make up the parish family.

APPLICATION. In what ways does our parish become aware of these connections with the diocese and the Universal Church? Confirmation, bishop's visitation, a visit to the cathedral, the diocesan newspaper, the seminary, a pilgrimage with other parishes to Rome.

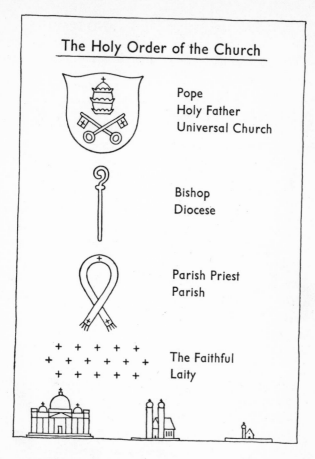

The Holy Order of the Church

Pope
Holy Father
Universal Church

Bishop
Diocese

Parish Priest
Parish

The Faithful
Laity

EXERCISE. Paste a photograph or make a drawing in your note-book of the Pope's church (St. Peter's, Rome), the cathedral church of your bishop, your own parish church.

50. THE CHURCH PROCLAIMS AND TEACHES

AIM. How the teaching of Christ is handed on, and those who hand it on: how the teaching office of the Church has its strength in the infallibility of the Pope.

PREPARATION. Who was it taught you about God and Christ? Parents, teachers, priests. All these are responsible to the bishop. The bishops are responsible to the Pope.

PRESENTATION. The proclamation of the dogma of the Assumption in 1950, at Rome. 700 Bishops from all over the world were gathered round the Pope.

EXPLANATION. The Pope consulted all the bishops of the world about the new dogma (Pope and bishops as teaching office), the decision of the Pope was the final step.

His infallibility as supreme teacher of the Church protected from error by the Holy Spirit. (Drawing: the Holy Spirit over St. Peter's.) All this must be clearly contrasted with the Pope speaking privately, e.g., in personal conversation at an Audience.

APPLICATION. A glance at the uncertainty, and therefore fickleness of human wisdom (Picture of a library, perhaps that of the teacher himself, with so many books on philosophy etc., and contrast these with the Holy Scriptures). The teaching office of the Church is the only place where no error is possible. This is the rock on which the Church is founded.

PLAY. A debate. Someone maintains that the infallibility of the Pope means that he cannot commit a sin. Explain what it really means.

The Church Teaches

Pope Bishops	}	Teaching Office

Priests Lay catechists Teachers Parents	}	Helpers

The Holy Spirit will teach you all things. (John 14:26)

Infallible ———— without error

Truth   Error

As the chief teacher of the Church (Dogma) - not as
a private person

51. THE CHURCH DRAWS HER TEACHING FROM HOLY SCRIPTURE AND FROM ORAL TRADITION

AIM. A close consideration of the sources of the Faith.

PRESENTATION. The parable of the householder who from his treasure brings forth new things and old (Matt. 13:52).

EXPLANATION. A treasure has been entrusted to the Church which contains everything and from which every teaching can be drawn. (Drawing of a treasure chest decorated with precious stones.) Inside it, the Holy Scriptures are to be found (O.T. – N.T.) and the writings of the Church Fathers who wrote down the sacred tradition (= oral tradition).

APPLICATION. The name of the most important books of the Old and New Testament must be learnt. Also learn to recognize the stamp of approval *(Imprimatur)*, which shows that it is a Catholic edition of the Bible. It is recommended that all quotations from Scripture written on the blackboard and in notebooks be cited with chapter and verse, the aim being to develop confidence and certainty in the use of the Bible.

EXERCISE. At home, look through your family Bible. Look for the *Imprimatur* and the year of its publication.

The Sources of the Faith

The Church is like a householder, who brings out
of his treasure chest things new and old.

Matt. 13:52

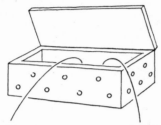

Holy Scripture   Oral Tradition

OT: Genesis = Psalms = Prophets

NT: Mt. Mk. Lk. Jo. Acts. Epistles - Apocalypse

Oral Tradition: Church Fathers (St. Augustine)

Imprimatur — Catholic edition of the Bible

When you pray, you speak to God —
when you read Holy Scripture, God speaks to you!

52. THE CHURCH'S MISSION TO PREACH EVERYWHERE

AIM. Helping the missions, as the personal duty of every Christian. Awake interest and enthusiasm, show the means.

PREPARATION. The teaching of Christ ought to be carried to the far corners of the earth, as he commanded: "Go into the whole world and preach the gospel to every creature" (Mark 16, 15).

PRESENTATION. Events, stories and reports from the mission field; material to be found in missionary magazines. Every teacher ought to collect and have ready a number of such reports and stories from the mission fields.

EXPLANATION. About one third of the human race is baptized: to win the rest for Christ is the task of the missionary bringing the message of Faith. Christ desires that these men also shall learn about him. Our love of Christ ought to show itself by an interest in his plans. The joyful news must be proclaimed to all mankind.

APPLICATION. How can I help? a. "The Pontifical Aid Society of the Holy Childhood" and its slogan, "All the world's children should be God's children". Encouragement and suggestions for the organization of such a group as this Pontifical Aid Society with a monthly contribution of five cents or a proposal to make a collection with a target of five dollars.

b. Give help by your daily prayers: One Hail Mary followed by "Holy Mary, Mother of God, pray for us and for all pagan children", (practice at the conclusion of several lessons).

c. It should be pointed out to the children that the work done in the missions is going to have an enormous influence in shaping the kind of world in which they will live as adults. For this reason alone, it should be taken very seriously.

The Missionary Task given by Christ

Go into the whole world and preach the Gospel
to every creature.   Mark 16:15

Mission = A Sending
A Missionary = A messenger
bringing the Faith

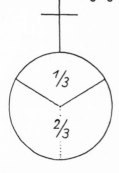

2 400 million men on the Earth
800 million men ($^1/_3$) are baptized

O Blessed Virgin Mary, pray for us and also
for pagan children!

EXERCISE. Write a letter to an African girl or boy, and explain
why the class is collecting money for his or her Baptism.

53. THE CHURCH CELEBRATES THE WORSHIP OF GOD

AIM. At the Holy Mass we become united with God.

PREPARATION. The threefold office of the Church: teaching office, priestly office, pastoral office. After the teaching office we now pass on to the priestly office.

PRESENTATION. A door both divides and connects. It is a barrier. So between God and us there is a mysterious, invisible door. God lives on the other side, we on this side. When the Church celebrates Mass this door is opened. We send up prayers, requests and gifts. In return God gives us an increase of grace, sacred food.

EXPLANATION. What is it that goes up to God and what comes down from God in return? 1. At devotions? (The ciborium in the drawing.) Recall various devotions: Stations of the cross, Benediction of the Blessed Sacrament, etc. From these arise worship and petition, while grace is given in return. 2. During a procession? (Drawing; a censer, e.g., Corpus Christi procession, once again worship and petition.) 3. At Holy Mass? (The chalice, the symbol for God the Father at the top of the drawing.) Sacrifice of praise, of thanksgiving, of petition and reparation. Rays descending from God the Father, symbol indicating the grace which comes down from God upon us.

APPLICATION. Search in your prayer books for the different religious services celebrated by the Church - Mass, Benediction, etc.

The most Holy Duty of the Church is

to Worship God

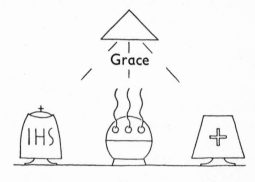

Grace

Benediction	Procession	Holy Mass
Adoration and Petition		Sacrifice Praise Thanksgiving Petition Reparation

54. THE CHURCH
ADMINISTERS THE HOLY SACRAMENTS

AIM. The seven sacraments as the sources of the grace-life. Their connection with Christ who won the key to them, and with the Church to whom they are entrusted. The underlying idea is that of a fountain of grace.

PREPARATION. Christ gave up his body and blood on the cross as a sacrifice. In return for this sacrifice he received the key to the sources of the grace-life. He entrusted this key into the keeping of the Church. How does she open up these sources of the grace-life?

PRESENTATION. A Roman fountain. A cross above and the seven openings in the bowl.

EXPLANATION. This is a comparison. From Christ on the cross flow living waters (= waters of life = the grace-life). The Church receives this wonderful treasure, as it were, into a great fountain and then distributes it through seven channels from which we can drink = the seven sacraments (enter their names in the same order as in the Catechism).

APPLICATION. The hymn "The Precious Blood" contains a verse which shows what the fountain of grace means for us:

> There the fainting spirit
> Drinks of life her fill;
> There as in a fountain
> Laves herself at will.

EXERCISE. Draw the symbols for the seven sacraments. Summarize, the external sign, the inner grace, foundation by Christ.

The Church distributes
the Holy Sacraments

THERE THE FAINTING SPIRIT
DRINKS OF LIFE HER FILL

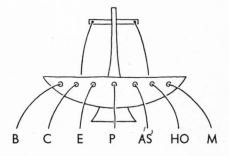

B   C   E   P   AS   HO   M

External sign
Inner Grace
Founded by Christ

55. THE CHURCH BLESSES AND CONSECRATES

AIM. The world of the sacramentals, their richness and position subordinate to the sacraments.

PREPARATION. Description of the two concepts, sacraments and sacramentals. Explanation of the difference between them: instituted by Christ, instituted by the Church.

PRESENTATION. The blessing with holy water of a rosary, cross or holy picture by a priest wearing a stole. This might be arranged during instruction.

EXPLANATION. A prayer of petition, holy water and a sign of the cross ("Nothing is feared by the evil spirit so much as the cross". - Cyril of Jerusalem), are the elements for a sacramental. When we raise our eyes to a blessed crucifix it helps us to believe and to pray, so that we may more earnestly call upon God to help us.

APPLICATION. Make a sketch of the sacramentals which accompany us through life: our parents' wedding rings, a crucifix in the house, holy water font, blessed candles, the blessing of St. Blaise, a palm from Palm Sunday, blessed bread at Easter, blessing of the bells, rosary, consecration of a church, blessing of a car, Paschal candle.

The Church blesses and consecrates

Sacraments — Sacramentals

Nothing is feared by the evil spirit so much as the cross. *Cyril of Jerusalem*

Instituted by the Church

56. THE PASTORAL TASK OF THE CHURCH

AIM. The parochial duties of their parish priest and curates provide the children with a very concrete picture of the pastoral task of the Church.

PREPARATION. Teaching office and priestly office – now a look at the pastoral office of the Church.

PRESENTATION AND EXPLANATION. Description of a day in the life of a priest. The individual duties are written on the blackboard, while attention is constantly drawn to the fact that it is with the care of souls that the priest is occupied day after day. A large, simple, wooden shepherd's crook shows how every activity of the priest is directed towards fulfilling his pastoral office. From the Epistle to Timothy: "Preach the word, be urgent in season, out of season; reprove, entreat, rebuke with all patience and teaching" (2 Tim. 4:2). How very difficult the priest finds it at times.

APPLICATION. Do you appreciate and sympathize with your priests? Sometimes they are mocked; what do you do when you hear such remarks? Let us all now say a silent prayer that God will help our priests in their difficult work.

Pastoral Task —— Care of Souls

—— Mass

—— Instruction

—— Preaching

—— Advising

—— House visiting

—— Care of the poor

—— Sick calls

—— Youth work

—— Confraternities

—— Teaching in school

St. Paul to Timothy: "Preach the word, be urgent in season, out of season; reprove, entreat, rebuke with all patience and teaching."

2 Tim. 4:2

57. THE CHURCH'S CARE
FOR ISOLATED CHRISTIANS

AIM. An insight into the difficulty of being alone in one's faith: an examination of our own ability on this point.

PREPARATION. How difficult it would be for our parish if we did not have a large church?

PRESENTATION. The kind of difficulties isolated Christians have to face: 1. Mass in a room or public hall. 2. Catholic children in non-Catholic schools: no Catholic friends for the family. 3. Dying without the sacraments.

EXPLANATION. The difficulties facing these isolated Christians: not having the company and support of other Catholics; surrounded by people who believe differently; or do not believe at all; under attack. (Drawing: the burning candle in the wind surrounded by extinguished candles.) They pass on the Faith; publicize it; attempt to rekindle it when it has been lost.

APPLICATION. How would I behave if suddenly I had to live under such conditions? Give thanks for the company of fellow Catholics who help me to believe. Readiness to help these isolated Christians: The Guild of Ransom. Perhaps the institution of a collection to help the Home Missions.

PLAY. A mechanic and an apprentice are repairing a car. The mechanic who has no religion makes fun of the Faith. "I believe only what I see." The Catholic apprentice tells him that he is wrong, and points out that electricity in a wire is invisible, so also radio waves and television waves.

Isolated Christians

To keep the Faith

      — alone

      — among unbelievers

      — under attack

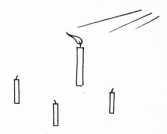

Guild of our Lady of Ransom - help for the
isolated Christians in our country

58. THE ONE TRUE CHURCH

AIM. A clear portrayal of the Catholic Church as alone founded by Christ and for this reason different from all other Christian religious groups.

PREPARATION. Most Catholic children come into contact with children who have been brought up as Protestants. What are we to make of them?

PRESENTATION. The college of cardinals comes together in Rome: from all parts of the earth, representatives of all those peoples who confess the same articles of Faith. They represent 400 million Catholics.

At an international congress at Evanston in 1954, there were representatives of 160 different religious denominations.

There was no unity whatsoever, not even a common form of worship.

EXPLANATION. What explains the unity of the Catholic Church? She stands on the rock upon which Christ founded her, his only Church: "Upon this rock I will build my Church." (Drawing: St. Peter's on the rock surrounded by tumultuous seas.)

The Catholic Church has also four marks or signs: One, Holy, Catholic, Apostolic. These are explained.

An examination is made of other Christian denominations, and it is pointed out that they lack these marks or signs, that though they may possess a part of the truth they have a great deal of error. The Catholic Church on the other hand possesses the whole truth. For these reasons we do not use the term "Church" when referring to other Christian denominations.

APPLICATION. What shall we think about them? How shall we behave towards them?

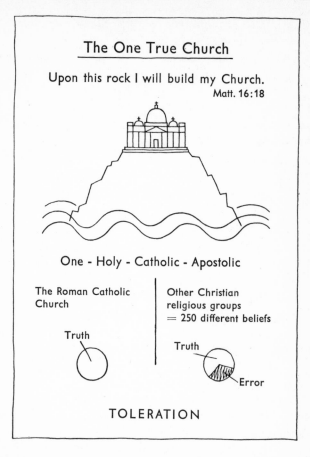

The One True Church

Upon this rock I will build my Church.
Matt. 16:18

One - Holy - Catholic - Apostolic

The Roman Catholic Church

Truth

Other Christian religious groups = 250 different beliefs

Truth

Error

TOLERATION

1. Concrete situations. A Catholic boy and a Protestant boy insult and deride each other. What is wrong about this?
2. Two children help a third who has met with an accident. On the way to the hospital they discover that they all have different

religions: (Catholic, Protestant, Jewish). Nevertheless, they continue to help. Respect for all men.

PLAY. 1. Mrs. Smith (Catholic) and Mrs. Jones (Protestant) buy their groceries in the shop of Mrs. Stern (Jewish). They are speaking about the above two situations. At the end they all agree: I keep to my own religion and I won't be persuaded otherwise. We have respect for each other and tolerate each other. At the conclusion the word toleration is explained and written on the blackboard.

2. The classroom is a court of law with judge and jury. Each religious group sends up a witness. He is questioned and the jury decides which of the four marks is lacking to the religious group to which he belongs.

3. Show your friend, by means of the globe, that the Catholic Church really is "catholic".

59. THE COMMUNION OF SAINTS

AIM. The three groups into which the whole people of God are divided, what they do for one another, and that on the Last Day they are to be united into one.

PREPARATION. What does the expression "the communion of saints" in the Creed mean?

PRESENTATION. The drawing. Three arcs of concentric circles whose center is the symbol for Christ, head of the Church. In the first are drawn the symbols of well known saints: e.g., bishop's mitre (= St. Nicholas); Mary's name symbol; key of heaven (= St. Peter); carpenter's ax (= St. Joseph); burning heart (= St. Augustine); harp (= St. Cecilia); tower (= St. Barbara). All these

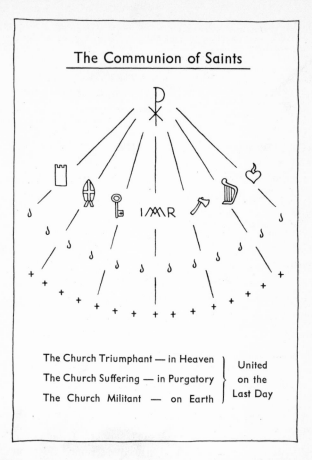

The Communion of Saints

The Church Triumphant — in Heaven   } United

The Church Suffering — in Purgatory   } on the

The Church Militant — on Earth   } Last Day

have conquered by their faith, they now belong to the Church Triumphant. In the second arc are drawn small red flames to represent the souls in purgatory. They are the Church Suffering. In the third arc small crosses stand for us Christians still on earth, and still fighting to win our eternal salvation: the Church Militant. Light from the Christus–symbol streams out and unites all three circles with Christ, making a "communion".

EXPLANATION. All three groups belong together, they form "the communion of saints" and they help each other. Those in heaven pray for us, and we pray for the souls in purgatory. We all wait for the Last Day when purgatory will cease to be, and there being no more divisions, we shall be united together with Christ as God's family.

APPLICATION. 1. This evening at night prayers each one ought to pray to a saint (perhaps his patron saint) and ask the saint to pray for him at God's throne.

2. Pray also this evening for a soul in purgatory: Lord have mercy on him, Christ have mercy on him, Lord have mercy on him.

3. Which saints would you ask for help in the following cases: in sickness, when making a dangerous journey, when looking for a good school, should your parents no longer go to Mass, for the conversion of a lapsed Catholic, in temptations against modesty or purity.

60. MARY IS OUR MOTHER AND OUR QUEEN

AIM. A picture of Mary drawn from the scriptures.

PREPARATION. Mary is most frequently found among our pictures of the Saints. What rank does she hold among the people of God?

PRESENTATION. The scripture citations about Mary are related and drawings are made. In addition – as a framework – the dogmas of the Immaculate Conception (stylized lilies) before birth, and of her

AVE MARIA

Mother of God
Queen of Heaven
Help of Christians

The Assumption

The Purification

The Visitation

The Annunciation

The Name of Mary

The Birth of Mary

The Immaculate Conception

SALVE REGINA

Pray for us, O Holy Mother of God, that we
may be made worthy of the promises of Christ

Assumption into heaven after death. The birthday of Mary (a
star shining over the waves); the name of Mary (the ancient
Christian name symbol for Mary); the Annunciation (the "Holy
Spirit will overshadow thee"); the Visitation (journey through

the mountains); the Purification (a sword will pierce thy heart).
EXPLANATION. From the events and the course of Mary's life
explain her three greatest titles: Mother of God, Queen of Heaven,
Help of Christians.

APPLICATION. The finest hymn to Our Lady (Salve Regina); and
the most important supplication to Our Lady (Pray for us, O holy
Mother of God, that we may be made worthy of the promises of
Christ); a beautiful picture of Our Lady (the teacher shows a
collection of various pictures of Our Lady, and encourages the
children to express their preference).

PLAY. Someone maintains that Catholics "adore" Our Lady. The
children give their answers.

61. CONVERSION TO GOD

AIM. As the conversion of an adult shows, our own membership of
the Church can never be taken for granted.

PREPARATION. It is a false idea to think that anyone can join the
Catholic Church as he would any other kind of society, by merely
signing his name. St. Jerome wrote:
"The body cannot take hold of the sacrament of Baptism if the soul
has not already accepted the truth of Faith." What does one have
to do when one wishes to become a Catholic?

PRESENTATION. Portrayal of the path to conversion: either a
classical example of a saint's conversion (e.g., St. Augustine), or
the normal path of an adult through several months instruction to
reception into the Church.

EXPLANATION. The steps along the way to Baptism are written
down: hearing; turning away (from false gods, "idols", e.g,.

Conversion to the Church

The body cannot take hold of the sacrament of Baptism if the soul has not already accepted the truth of Faith.   *St. Jerome*

At the Crossroads

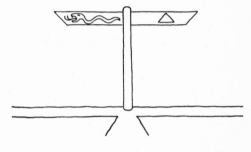

False Gods	The One True God,
Idols	the Father
Error	of Our Lord
Sin	Jesus Christ

Hearing → Turning Away → Conversion → Baptism

pleasures, errors, sin); conversion (the personal decision at the crossroads to believe in the one, true God, the Father of Our Lord Jesus Christ); only then follows the reception into the Church by Baptism.

43

APPLICATION. 1. What kind of a fate is in store for anyone who through his own fault chooses not to believe? A terrible one!

2. Name several kinds of "idols" (the false gods of today) loved by men more than they love God.

DISCUSSION. What answer would you give to the following often-heard saying: "It doesn't matter what you believe, but it is what you are that counts?" – Edward says, "I would not become a Catholic, I know so many bad ones." What would you answer?

62. THE RITE OF BAPTISM

AIM. The essential facts of Baptism, to be well instilled.

PREPARATION. A Baptism lasts fifteen minutes. There is much to be seen. We are going to deal with only the essentials.

PRESENTATION AND EXPLANATION. An adult comes for Baptism. First he must make a vow, the baptismal vow. Then follows the most important part, the pouring of the water over his head and the speaking of the words of Baptism. (Drawing: Baptismal font and the little cruet from which water is poured.)

APPLICATION. Everyone should know how to baptize in an emergency. Holy water is a reminder of our Baptism.

The Giving of Baptism

Baptismal Vow
Pouring of Water
Words of Baptism

I baptize you in the name
of the Father
and of the Son
and of the Holy Ghost.

Baptism in case of need

62a. THE SOLEMN BAPTISM OF CHILDREN

AIM. A picture of the complete ceremony of Baptism: prominence given to secondary rites.

PREPARATION. You are to be the God-parent of a small child. What do you have to do at the ceremony?

PRESENTATION. The teacher goes through a mock Baptism; someone is chosen to be God-parent; for the child a white cloth can be used.

EXPLANATION. The important elements are dwelt upon and explained: The God-parent (his duty); name of the child (patron saint); "Depart from him" (a word about Exorcism. The child is delivered from the power of the evil spirits); "Ephpheta!" (be opened – faith is a grace); the threefold pouring in form of a cross (Drawing); the white baptismal garment (the wedding garment = the grace-life); the burning candle (Christ the light! Point out the connection with the Easter light).

APPLICATION. Learn the answers that the God-parent gives, and thus see more clearly what vows were made for you at Baptism.

Baptism of a Child

God parents
Patron Saint
"Depart from him"
"Ephpheta!"

The wedding
garment

Christ, the
Light!

63. BAPTISM IS THE SOURCE OF NEW LIFE

AIM. Under the title "To be born again", the supernatural character of grace-life is emphasized.

PREPARATION. A sacrament has an outward sign, gives inner grace, is instituted by Jesus Christ. What is the inner grace given at Baptism?

PRESENTATION. The Nicodemus scene with particular emphasis on the words "Unless a man be born again of water and the Spirit he cannot enter into the Kingdom of God" (John 3: 1–5).

EXPLANATION. To be born = to receive life from one's father and mother. To be born again from God (= from the Father) and from water (= from the Church) gives life (= grace-life). Drawing: a human heart between water and the Holy Spirit. The stain inherited at the first birth is wiped out (original sin); the grace-life with its powers (faith, hope, charity = theological virtues) flows into the heart. The reality of this new birth shows itself in a new relationship to God the Father (child of God), to God the Son (brother and sister of Jesus), and to the Holy Spirit (Temple of the Holy Spirit).

APPLICATION. Is there anyone in your family or among your friends of whom you can say that he or she has been or has not been "born again"?

The new Birth

from water and the spirit

Original sin — grace-life — theological virtues

In the name
of the Father   — child of God
of the son   — brother and sister of Jesus
of the Holy Spirit — Temple of the Holy Spirit

64. FAITH

AIM. Concentration on that part of the virtue of faith which is more easily understood by children, namely: Whom I am to believe. The interconnection between Church, Christ, and God, must be deeply impressed.

PREPARATION. The grace-life brings with it divine powers: faith, hope, and charity. What effect has the virtue of faith on those baptized?

PRESENTATION. The Baptism of the Ethiopian by Philip, from the Acts of the Apostles (Acts 8: 26–40).

EXPLANATION. a. The Ethiopian in meeting the apostle Philip was in fact meeting the Church. Through the apostle he was led to the Son of God who brought the joyful news from the Father. This trinity of Church, Christ, and God, must be clearly pointed out and committed to memory from the blackboard summary.
b. The teaching of the Church brings together what God has revealed. It is the truth. The believer holds fast to this truth.

APPLICATION. The power of the virtue of faith has been planted in me like a small seed. Whoever, while he is still a child and a youth, does not foster and protect this faith, will never have the strength to believe when he comes into contact with the unbelieving world. Concluding prayer: "Increase my faith, fix all my hopes on thee, and bind my heart to thine in deathless charity."

DISCUSSION. John has been learning the Catechism for three years and now thinks he knows his Faith – what do you say to that? Can divine truths ever become old fashioned?

The Faith

Who hears the Church — hears Christ,
Who hears Christ — hears God!

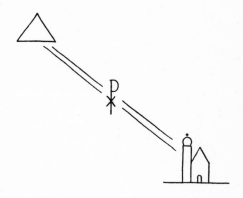

Revelation = Truth

65. THE LIFE OF FAITH

AIM. To convey some understanding of the dangers to faith and to instill an attitude of vigilance.

PREPARATION. The flower of faith in the garden of the soul. It has to grow, to be protected and taken care of, to receive nourishment. Dangers: hoar-frost, insufficient nourishment.

PRESENTATION. The life of a martyr, e.g., St. Catherine, making clear the choice which was put before her: Apostacy or Loyalty.

EXPLANATION. a. The two extremes are made clear through explanation and picture. Apostacy (burning incense before the false gods); loyalty even unto death (martyrs' victory symbols). b. Even though our faith may never be put to this severe test, yet lesser dangers often bring before us the choice of apostacy or loyalty: difficulties in belief (e.g., whether Jesus had brothers in the flesh); temptations against faith (e.g. "It was all made up by the priests"); doubts (e.g., The bread does not really become the body and blood of Christ).

It depends on the ability of the children whether these ideas are merely mentioned or entered into more deeply with further examples and how they are dealt with. The teacher should formulate these examples so that they appear as difficulties, temptations and doubts.

APPLICATION. Examination of conscience, first point of examination: prayer. My prayer-life will show whether my faith is strong or weak. Prayer is the barometer of my faith.

DISCUSSION. Is John right when he says, "Good habits are the muscles of the soul, the more one exercises them the stronger they become"? Show the truth of this, for example, in daily prayer, in going to Sunday Mass, in going often to the sacraments.

My Life of Faith

Growth — development — protection — confession

| Apostacy | Loyal confession of |
| Denial of faith | the faith |

Difficulties in belief — Temptations against faith

Doubts in belief

66. HOPE

AIM. It needs a lifetime's experience to fully grasp the meaning and value of hope. Children do not have this experience. One can only seek to give them a strong image (the saving anchor) of the virtue of hope, the full meaning of which will only later become apparent.

PREPARATION. Today we are to learn about a power that was born in the depths of our soul at Baptism. We shall need to rely on this power later when the stormy seas of trouble and difficulty crash into our life.

PRESENTATION. Portrayal (perhaps in common with the children) of a ship caught in a storm. The only hope is the anchor which prevents the ship from being hurled on to a reef (Drawing).

EXPLANATION. It often happens this way to the ship of our life. At such times we also need an anchor which can save us. For example:

a. A school friend is ill, he has to remain in bed for a whole summer. He is very depressed. Where can he find the strength to put up with this? Hope for good health gives him patience; he often begs God to let him get well again soon. He holds on to this prospect of a return to good health as though it were an anchor (Hope for earthly benefits).

b. A motorcyclist has a bad accident, and the doctor tells him he will not live much longer. In what can he find strength to bring him through these last painful hours of his life? A priest speaks to him of God, who forgives sins and gives eternal happiness. After a hard struggle he lets down this anchor to keep the ship of his life steady, and he dies in peace (Hope for heavenly benefits).

c. Very often a terrible fate overtakes some men. Terrible suf-

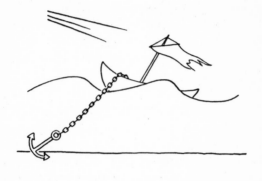

Our Hope

Worldly goods — Heavenly goods

I hope for the return of Christ
in power and majesty

... who strengthens us in hope!

ferings come upon innocent people, our faith is shaken (famine, war, plague, political persecution). So often there remains only one anchor: the hope in the return of Christ on the Last Day, when he will take from the evil ones their powers (= core of all hope).

APPLICATION. Hope is a great power which is meant to grow within us. We will pray to God that he will make it strong in us: "Increase my faith, fix all my hopes on thee, and bind my heart to thine in deathless charity."

PLAY. a. A visit to a sick friend. He complains impatiently that he is missing all the fun, swimming, games, etc. The visitor seeks to console him.

b. Your elder brother is thrown out of work and sits at home very depressed. What do you say to him?

c. A girl's mother dies. She is inconsolable. You go with her to her mother's grave. How can you console her?

67. LOVE FOR GOD

AIM. The virtue of charity is certainly the most difficult subject in which to give instruction. If the teacher aims at stimulating devotional experience it most often fails to materialize. It is therefore advisable to handle this subject quite factually. Often a devotional experience takes place spontaneously.

PREPARATION. A heart is drawn on the blackboard. What does it stand for? A symbol of love; to have a heart; to be heartless. The world would be a very chilly place if there were no love in it.

PRESENTATION AND EXPLANATION. What kind of a heart has God? We can find out from what he does. God the Father: he has created me, lets me live, has sent his Son to us and keeps his Kingdom ready for us; all this draws me to love my most mysterious Creator. "I love you, God the Father." (Blackboard.) God the Son: who brought to us the joyful news; who died on the cross for us: his heart was pierced right through (Drawing: the wound

GOD IS LOVE

I love you, God the Father

I love you, God the Son

I love you, God the Holy Spirit

in the heart and the cross behind the heart); how ought we to love him? Above all things? God the Holy Spirit: who works in our soul, so that the grace-life and the divine powers of faith, hope and charity grow in us, who dwells within us, who unites us with

God; give him also a word of love even though we do not know him.

APPLICATION. He shows his love of God best who lets his love stream out upon his fellow men. (Drawing: Cross with golden rays. This design on the blackboard reminds us to bestow the love of God on others.) It is a good idea to complete the lesson with a description of the work of some Catholic charitable organizations, e.g., Society of St. Vincent de Paul, and how we might support it. This will serve, as it were, as a protective envelope for the main theme – love for God. It is also recommended that the prayer of love for God written on the blackboard be prayed in silence during the closing prayers.

68. LOVE FOR OUR NEIGHBOR

AIM. Strong portrayal of the situation in which a fellow-man becomes my neighbor. The great responsibility of loving our neighbor.

PREPARATION. One can find out the temperature by looking at a thermometer; how the weather has changed by looking at a barometer. One can also find out how much we love God by seeing how much we love our neighbor. So close together are these loves, that love of our neighbor is a barometer which shows how much we love God. It is very bad if they are not found together. It is, therefore, very important to know exactly what love for our neighbor means.

PRESENTATION. The story of the Good Samaritan (Luke 10:30–37).

EXPLANATION. What is repeated three times? 1. A man lies there in need. 2. Another sees him. 3. It is possible for him to help. In

LOVE OF NEIGHBOR

Fellow man ──────→ sees need

helps
_____

my neighbor

Go and do you also in like manner.

Luke 10:37

Without exception: Color - language - religion - enemy

THE GOLDEN RULE

this moment he becomes his neighbor. That is the meaning of
Jesus' command: "Go and do also in like manner" - as the Good
Samaritan.

There are no exceptions to this command: color, race, language, religion, even an enemy. ("But I say to you, love your enemies", Matt. 5:44.) Because Jesus feels it, it is a terrible thing if a Christian does not practise love of his neighbor. ("As long as you did not do it for one of these least ones . . .", Matt. 25:40–45.)

APPLICATION. 1. The golden rule from the catechism lesson.

2. Our attitude towards our fellow-men: respect, politeness, friendliness, thoughtfulness, care.

3. The story of St. Martin. His cloak and his dream (drawing).

4. A conference in the classroom: a representative comes from each race (color), perhaps wearing some characteristic sign or costume. On the agenda: a. election of a president, b. the foundation of the International Red Cross.

5. Discussion: A certain Christian claims that he loves God but shows no sign of loving his neighbor. What effect does such a one have? A certain Catholic practises love of neighbor, but does not go to church. What are we to think of him?

6. Play: The victim of an accident lies on the road. Two motorists in a large car dive past. (They sit on two chairs before the class.) The owner of the car does not want to stop; the other pursuades him to pull up. The arguments used by both are very important.

7. The International Red Cross. Their work in the event of a major catastrophy.

69. FOLLOWING CHRIST

AIM. Whoever follows Christ comes also into contact with the cross. How Christ bore his cross: first initiation into the rewarding secret of the cross.

PREPARATION. Our way through life (from birth until death); Jesus' way through life, a part of which was the way of the cross (drawing). But Jesus said we have to "follow" him: does that mean that we also have to walk the way of the cross?

PRESENTATION. The words of Jesus: "And he who does not carry his cross . . ." (Luke 14:27).

EXPLANATION. 1. What are the crosses men have to carry? Pain, sickness, suffering, poverty, evil persons, a drunken father, a brother turned thief. The word cross is here used metaphorically, and means all the unpleasant things that can happen to me.

2. How do men usually carry their cross? With much complaining, with resentment, with indifference, blaming God, with patience, bravely, with a sad heart, with a joyful heart.

3. How did Jesus carry his cross? Voluntarily, bravely, he knew its secret: by means of the cross, he is able to help and save us. (The illuminated Christus-symbol in the summary.) It gave him so much power. The cross will also help us if we carry it as Jesus did (e.g., that someone ill will be restored to health; that a lapsed Catholic will return to his duties; that someone will be converted; that all my sins will be forgiven). That is a great secret of the cross. When a man imitates Christ in this way, then is he a follower of Christ.

4. For Christians there is sometimes a special cross: being made fun of because he is a Christian (goes to church). Maybe he loses his job, or is even persecuted. Then he is suffering as Christ did.

Some, indeed, have had an actual cross to carry. (Peter, Andrew, and other martyrs both in the past and at present.)

5. If, on our journey through life, we have to go by the way of the cross as Jesus did, there is at the end of it a goal of which he often spoke: perfection. This means that in all our actions, our thoughts, and in our speech we become wholly like Jesus.

APPLICATION. 1. Reference to the book, *The Imitation of Christ*.

2. A saying of Leo the Great: "We bear the name of Christ in vain if we are not also followers of Christ." What do those people do who refuse to carry their cross?

3. Where can each of us find his cross? Be still and reflect! Very quietly we will now tell Christ in prayer whether we wish to carry our cross as he did.

4. Discussion: If my parents do not wish to let me go to church, what ought I to do?

FOLLOWING CHRIST

He who does not carry his cross and
follow me cannot be my disciple.

Luke 14:27

A Christian is one who follows Christ

PERFECTION

70. JESUS TEACHES US TO PRAY

AIM. Teaching on prayer is a constant theme throughout all religious instruction, each lesson should add a new piece to the ever growing pattern.

Here we are concerned with three points only: What is due to God and what man has need of, in prayer: also the definition of prayer: the raising of the heart and mind to God.

PREPARATION. Bodily breathing and its necessity. How does the soul breathe? "Prayer is the breath of the soul."

PRESENTATION. Jesus teaches us to pray. The two kinds of petition in the Our Father: what is due to God; what we have need of.

EXPLANATION. During prayer we raise our eyes, hands, thoughts, in short our heart to God above: praying means raising your heart to God. Sursum corda! (Drawing.)

APPLICATION. My prayer books: simple book of prayers, the missal. The prayers I know by heart. My own, personal, not made-up prayer.

PLAY. A mime: getting up in the morning, from rising till school time. References to morning prayer can be brought in quite easily according to the way in which the mime is played: morning prayers forgotten, lazy or neglectful execution, the various possibilities of prayer, etc.

Jesus teaches us to Pray

Our Father

What is due to God	What we need
3 petitions	4 petitions

To pray means to raise one's heart to God

Sursum Corda!

 Prayer book

Missal

71. HOW WE SHOULD PRAY

AIM. Recollection as the greatest aid to prayer.

PREPARATION. A prayer must have various characteristics: devoutness (incense-like prayer: our thoughts are like the tiny grains of incense). Prayer that is not devout is like an empty coffee grinder, turning but having no coffee beans to grind. Full of trust (God will help); persevering (keep on knocking). Recollection is of the greatest help in achieving all these.

PRESENTATION. The words of Jesus: "But when you pray, go into your room, and closing your door, pray to your Father in secret; and your Father, who sees in secret, will reward you." (Matt. 6:6).

EXPLANATION. What does Jesus mean by that? First the external situation: to be alone in order not be distracted by others, etc., not to show off. However, if our thoughts are roaming everywhere, we might just as well be in the street as in our room; on the other hand, in a street or in a crowd one can be as if alone in one's room: alone with God. "Into your room" is a metaphor and means recollection: to have my heart alone with God. Then will our prayer be right. (The drawing has the ancient Christian symbol for the soul opened out towards God.)

APPLICATION. What have I to do to become recollected? a. Collect my thoughts, bring them away from everything else; concentration upon my intention: I want to speak to God; wait until all is quiet within me.

b. Attitude. Standing, kneeling, lying (in bed: many children are only alone when in bed; therefore this position may be regarded as helpful. The children are indeed very grateful for any instruction which shows them how to conceal their praying from the gaze

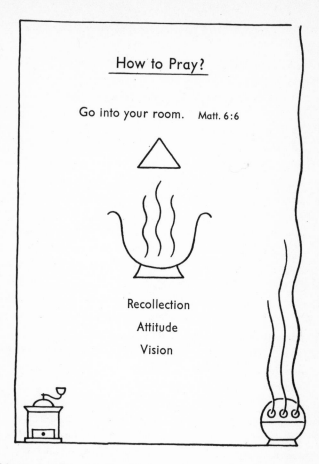

How to Pray?

Go into your room.   Matt. 6:6

Recollection

Attitude

Vision

of family and friends); sitting (at the table: how can one say grace, so that the others do not notice?).

c. The various positions for the hands.

d. Vision. Look at a crucifix, a picture, towards heaven, the eyes closed.

PLAY. The parable of the importunate friend (Luke 11:5-8).

72. THE ARRANGING OF PRAYER

AIM. From the Catechism text, two sections are chosen and each considered in one lesson.

1. Prayer at home. 2. Prayer in church.

PREPARATION. The clock tells us when it is time for school. There is also another time-keeper, which once told the time for the soul: the cock.

PRESENTATION. Why do we often see a weather-cock on a church spire? It is a reminder of the cock which crowed when St. Peter betrayed Christ. It reminds us of Christ's warning "Watch and pray". The cock, however, was, in the early days, regarded as an alarm clock. It used to cry out at dawn, the time for prayer, and it summoned the people to early Mass. Thus the cock on the church spire reminds us also of the daily order.

EXPLANATION. Each day has its order, morning and evening, beginning and end. Both should be united to God by prayer, morning prayer and evening prayer.

During the day the cock warns us: "watch and pray!" Also when in need and in danger (e.g., when crossing the roads; signified in the drawing by the red traffic signal – "Watch out, danger!"), in temptation (e.g., staying out late at night, keeping bad company: or visiting a bad movie: the serpent as symbol of temptation). It is a good idea to prepare ejaculatory prayers for such situations.

APPLICATION. Seek out an ejaculatory prayer from the Catechism text, or make one up to be said in times of need and when tempted.

Watch and Pray

The daily prayers

Ejaculatory prayer

When danger threatens   In temptation

72a. PRAYER IN CHURCH

AIM. A clear distinction is to be made between private and communal prayer in the church.

PREPARATION. Many people say: "I do not go to Mass, because there is too much distraction. I can pray better alone." Is this right?

PRESENTATION. a. The teacher describes a private visit to the Blessed Sacrament (in the drawing, the sanctuary lamp). There one is alone before God: a typical prayer at this time is: "My Lord and My God."

b. Holy Communion for all follows on the celebration of the Eucharist. We are invited together. We are not there on our own initiative but on the invitation of Christ who invites us all to a common table. A typical prayer for this occasion is, "Gratias agamus Domino Deo nostro" (in the drawing, the altar with the congregation assembled in rows). Of course the celebration of the Mass must be done correctly, i.e., the periods of silence during the Canon and after the Communion must be observed.

c. Justification of both kinds of prayer; each has its proper time.

APPLICATION. Encourage private visits to the Blessed Sacrament, practice the Mass responses in both Latin and English. Speak about the periods of silence during a dialogue Mass.

DISCUSSION. Explain to a non-Catholic friend why the sanctuary lamp is always kept burning.

In the Church

Alone
before
God

My Lord
and
my God!

All
together
before
God

Gratias
agamus
Domino
Deo nostro

73. THE RITE OF CONFIRMATION

Instruction preparatory to the sacrament of Confirmation is usually given outside the normal religion curriculum. The two lessons in the Catechism provide exemplary matter for review immediately before the reception of the sacrament. However, just as the lesson for First Communion is followed by very full instruction in the Holy Sacrifice of the Mass, so it is advisable here also to review Confirmation within the framework of the teaching on the sacraments. This is particularly important when the sacrament of Confirmation has been received at an early age.

AIM. The external sign of Confirmation.

PREPARATION. A rubber stamp and the impression it makes correspond to each other. One can read on the stamp the impression it will make. It is like this with the sacraments. The external sign stands for something which cannot be seen. Let us now examine what the external sign can tell us.

PRESENTATION. The great ceremony with the bishop present, to whom all come, shows that something is expected from those about to be confirmed. The bishop himself requires from them the renewal of their baptismal vows, and he takes their promises very seriously. At the laying on of hands, the candidate for Confirmation comes into contact with the great stream of power which is transmitted from Christ through the apostles to the bishops. The anointing with holy oil gives power and strength to body and soul so that they may perform a definite task. (Drawing: saucer and the oil vase.) The whole external sign points to a strengthening for a definite task. Confirmation means a strengthening.

APPLICATION. Go through the baptismal vows from a Holy Week

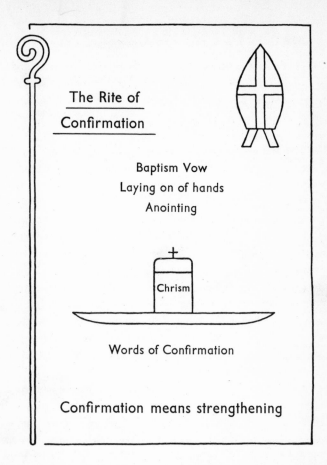

The Rite of Confirmation

Baptism Vow
Laying on of hands
Anointing

Chrism

Words of Confirmation

Confirmation means strengthening

manual. Prayer: examination of conscience and silent renewal of baptismal promises.

74. THE GRACE OF CONFIRMATION

AIM. The strengthening given by the grace of Confirmation enables us to fulfil the task of living in the world as active Christians, in particular in the concrete circumstances and surroundings of our everyday life, and of exerting on them a Christian influence through all the means at our disposal.

This task is illustrated by the gospel event in which Jesus appears at the Jordan – leaving behind his hidden life in order to begin his public work.

PREPARATION. On our way through life we move along in stages. One period in our life comes to an end and a new one begins, e.g., we start school; we leave school to learn a trade or profession; the period of training ends and we become qualified. Always we are moving upwards by stages, and each new stage brings a new task and responsibility. (Often the passing from one stage to another is celebrated: when we start school or leave school, our 21st birthday or when we have been fully trained in our job, when we are married, etc.) It was just the same for Christ: When he was twelve years old; and particularly when his hidden life came to an end and he began his public life.

PRESENTATION. The scene at the Jordan when Jesus was baptized. He who was without sin was immersed in the same water in which men had symbolically tried to wash away their sins: he was showing them that he intended to take these sins upon himself. "He drew on himself the sinful slime of the Jordan", as a Christian author puts it. He is now ready to begin his public task: the salvation of the world. As he stepped out of the water, the heavens opened and the Father acknowledged him and strengthened him with the Holy Spirit. From this moment he set about his

The Grace of Confirmation

private life

public life

To make the world Christian!

public work; a new stage in his life had begun. (Diagrammatic representation of this scene in the drawing).

EXPLANATION. This is a parallel to what happens at Confirmation. Here we declare that we intend to live as Christians;

75

then the bishop, reflecting a little of the glory of God the Father, comes to us and, by the laying on of his hands and the anointing, strengthens us with the Holy Spirit for a new task in life. What is this task? Exactly the same as Christ's! To do something in the world, to change it and refashion it; in a word, to make it Christian. For this task Confirmation strengthens us with the Holy Spirit.

APPLICATION. This we can do of course only in our own surroundings, and with the means we as school children possess; e.g., get a school friend to go regularly to Mass.

PLAY. A family scene. Sunday morning before the childrens' Mass. Father reads the paper, his daughter plays with a doll and hums a hit tune; her brother is busy with his stamp collection; mother prepares a meal. The boy says: "It is time for Mass." The father replies, "Nothing doing, you're staying at home." Imagine you are the brother and sister. What would you reply?

75. JESUS CHRIST INSTITUTED THE HOLY EUCHARIST

Instruction on the Mass should be given every year after the reception of First Holy Communion. The five lessons which follow provide a systematic digest of eucharistic doctrine, as well as a framework for those truths which every Catholic must know.

AIM. The following topics are dealt with together: the institution of the Holy Eucharist, the consecration of the species, and the consecrating power of the priest.

PREPARATION. One often sees in museums beautifully-written ancient documents bearing many seals, e.g., from medieval kings. Many of them are royal charters, in which one can study how a

The Last Supper

1. The words of Foundation:

"A meal"

2. Consecration:

bread ———→ body
wine ———→ blood

"The Species"

3. Authority:

Ordination

---

town became self-governing. Particularly interesting are thousand year old documents which are still valid today: e.g., the foundation of a hospital or a university college. What they set down is still in effect today. Such an interesting document is the account of the Last Supper; almost two thousand years old and yet still in effect today.

PRESENTATION. One or two accounts from the Scriptures (1 Cor. 11:23–25; Luke 22:19–20).

EXPLANATION. 1. The "foundation-account" is first portrayed as an important document on which for almost 2,000 years each Holy Mass is founded; in every church, in every part of the world. 2. The foundation was made during the course of a meal, so that even today the external sign of the Holy Mass represents a meal. (Drawing: paten, bread and chalice on either side of the Christus-symbol). 3. The words of consecration said by Jesus express a wonderful changing of the bread and wine by which the outer form remains the same. Unlike the changing of the water into wine, the outer form of the bread and wine remain the same. They are the "containers" which hide and protect their precious contents. 4. Expressly, Christ made the foundation with the words: "Do this. . . ." This power has been handed down, like an unbroken chain, to every Catholic priest in the world. (Drawing: Christus-symbol, key for the apostles, shepherd's staff for the bishops, a crossed green stole for the priests.)

APPLICATION. What are the different attitudes, of both mind and body, of people present at the Holy Mass? Which attitude have you at Mass? Which do you think is the best attitude of mind and body?

76. THE CHURCH
CELEBRATES THE HOLY EUCHARIST

AIM. The Mass and the Last Supper are identical.

PREPARATION. Have you ever seen old editions of the gospels? The

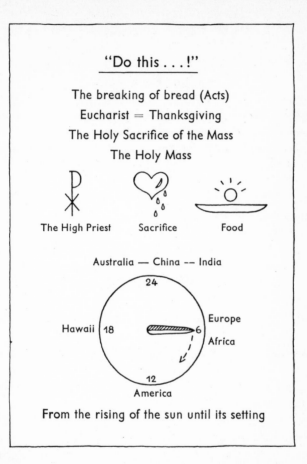

"Do this . . . !"

The breaking of bread (Acts)

Eucharist = Thanksgiving

The Holy Sacrifice of the Mass

The Holy Mass

The High Priest   Sacrifice   Food

Australia — China –– India

Hawaii   18   24   6   Europe

Africa

12

America

From the rising of the sun until its setting

printing, the paper, and the binding are all different. The contents, however, remain the same. It has been just like this with the Mass through the centuries. The outer form has changed, the inner content has remained the same.

PRESENTATION. Let us prove this by comparing the Last Supper with the Mass said in our church. Here are two pictures. Let us silently look at them. (A picture of the Last Supper is now shown, and perhaps a photograph of the parish Mass.)

EXPLANATION. What is different? Go through all the externals (Room – church; everyday clothes – vestments; eating utensils – chalice, etc.). The name has also changed: Last Supper – the breaking of bread – Eucharist – Holy Mass. But what has remained the same? The High Priest, the sacrificial Victim (Body and Blood of Christ), and the food. (Drawing.)

APPLICATION. A Mass clock. From the rising of the sun until its setting the Holy Mass is celebrated.

77. IN THE CELEBRATION OF HOLY EUCHARIST THE SACRIFICE OF THE CROSS IS MADE PRESENT

AIM. The renewal of the Sacrifice of Calvary in the Sacrifice of the Mass.

PREPARATION. How are precious things protected? For example, precious jewels are kept in a decorative casket which is kept safe and under cover. In the Holy Mass there is a mystery concealed as though behind a veil.

PRESENTATION. The Eucharist is a communal meal: first the table is prepared, then follows a kind of grace before meals (Canon) spoken by the priest alone. During this prayer something happens. A high point is reached at the consecration. We have already learnt about it: the priest speaks the words that Christ spoke and does what Christ did at the Last Supper. Then the bells ring and the priest genuflects showing us the holy species of bread and

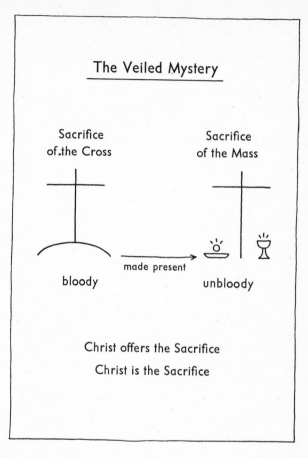

The Veiled Mystery

Sacrifice
of the Cross

Sacrifice
of the Mass

made present →

bloody

unbloody

Christ offers the Sacrifice

Christ is the Sacrifice

wine, which are now changed. All this indicates that something of great importance has happened.

EXPLANATION. Behind it all there is a mystery so hidden that one cannot see it: veiled as it were. What takes place invisibly is a sacrifice offered by Christ; the same one in fact as that made on the first Good Friday, when he offered his body and blood on the cross. Body and blood under the form of bread and wine are the signs of this sacrifice.

Now the Church teaches us: The Sacrifice of the Cross and the Sacrifice of the Mass are one and the same sacrifice. The Sacrifice of the Cross is made present in the Sacrifice of the Mass: present with all its power, saving, making reparation, and giving worship to God the Father. In both, Christ is the High Priest and the Victim. There is only one difference. On the cross the sacrifice was for Christ bloody and painful; at the Holy Mass it is unbloody. (Drawing: Calvary with cross; Holy Mass with paten and chalice under the cross. A large arrow between.) All this is a great mystery. The Canon of the Holy Mass is like a veil behind which the mystery is concealed. Christ wished it to be so, since at the Last Supper he said: "Do this . . .!" i.e., do what is being done here. You now understand why instead of the Holy Mass we can say the Holy Sacrifice of the Mass.

APPLICATION. How do we conduct ourselves during the consecration? Sign of the Cross: "My Lord and My God", lowering the head? Or better: look up at the holy species and pray, "Accept O Holy Father, the body of Our Lord Jesus Christ who for us was sacrificed on the cross – Accept O Holy Father, the blood of Our Lord Jesus Christ which was shed for us on the cross."

78. IN THE EUCHARISTIC MEAL WE RECEIVE THE BREAD OF ETERNAL LIFE

AIM. The first instruction of this Catechism lesson is concerned with three points:

1. The power which Holy Communion has for eternal life.

2. The union with Christ.

3. Help in the struggle against sin and error.

PREPARATION. The very carefully prepared food given to sportsmen. Quite definite powers are expected from this nourishment, just like the special rations one takes on a long walking or climbing tour. The nourishment given at Mass also has a very definite effect on both body and soul.

PRESENTATION AND EXPLANATION. 1. The words of Jesus: "He who eats my flesh . . . has life everlasting and I will raise him up on the Last Day." A most mysterious power lies in this holy bread: powers of resurrection, life-powers as in the resurrected Christ. 2. In this holy food many mysteries are hidden. One of them we remember from our First Holy Communion: Jesus comes into my heart. Is that not a wonderful thing: someone with whom I am able to speak comes deep inside me. My heart becomes the dwelling of Jesus. How must I prepare myself? Communion means being united with someone.

3. We now speak of a third effect of the holy food. We can compare our soul to a garden in which grow both flowers (our good habits and virtues) and weeds (our bad habits and sins). Holy Communion acts like a wonderful sun. Everything good grows greater, everything bad grows less, in fact the soul is made clean of all venial sins. We can say: Holy Communion increases the grace-life in us.

APPLICATION. I. Devotion at Communion. Let us decide to think about one of its three effects the next time we receive Holy Communion.

1. I will keep myself quite still and let the powers of resurrection in my body and soul penetrate deeper.

2. I will greet Jesus as a guest in my heart and make up my mind exactly what I am going to say to him.

3. I will beg the wonderful divine power in the holy bread to cleanse me from the sins of the past week, to help in the coming week, e.g., in my dealings with others.

At the end draw the following symbols: Wheat (= the holy food); the banner of resurrection (= the powers of resurrection); a heart in the Christus-symbol (= for the union with Christ); and the sun (its rays shining on the garden of the soul).

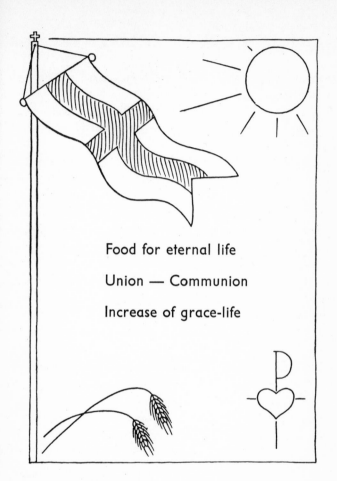

Food for eternal life

Union — Communion

Increase of grace-life

78a. THE CONDITIONS FOR FREQUENT COMMUNION

AIM. Incitement to more frequent Communion, perhaps even every Sunday.

PREPARATION. Do you stay away from Holy Communion when you have committed venial sins? Yes-No? What does the Church say about this?

PRESENTATION. The decree of St. Pius X on Holy Communion, with its invitation to more frequent, even daily, Communion.

Since it was made, something like a new Spring has passed through the whole Church. At every Holy Mass there is an invitation to more frequent Communion. People no longer confine themselves to the minimum: once in the year.

EXPLANATION. St. Pius X, however, laid down certain conditions. First condition: I must be in a state of grace, i.e., I must be in possession of the grace-life. Only through a mortal sin can it be lost. We shall soon be hearing more about mortal sin. Whoever goes to Communion in mortal sin makes an unworthy Communion. He is eating the holy bread without having the grace-life. Christ has forbidden that! Whoever does so, and is aware of what he is doing, commits a terribly great sin.

Second condition: Whoever goes often to Communion must have the right intentions; that means that there is also a wrong intention (e.g., in order to impress the priest and others). Those with these intentions should keep away from Communion. The right intention, however, would be: I want to have more powers of resurrection in me; I want to speak more to Jesus within me; I want to be helped more and more by the power of the holy bread. Such a person is like one who has a lamp burning: he is

The Invitation

1. In the state of grace

2. The right intention

Worthy — unworthy Communion

Fasting

taking care to have plenty of oil for his lamp (Drawing of lamp. Recall the parable of the wise virgins).

APPLICATION. Consider what your intentions are!

Now let us speak about fasting. Many stay away from Communion on account of the fasting. Is that right? Speak about the new fasting regulations. It is particularly important to point out that water does not break the fast.

79. HONORING OUR LORD IN THE BLESSED SACRAMENT

AIM. An appreciative understanding of the reservation and benediction of the Blessed Sacrament.

PREPARATION. Compare a Protestant and a Catholic church. The sanctuary lamp, the presence of Christ in the holy bread. God is continually present in a Catholic church.

PRESENTATION. The consecration, during Mass, of the hosts for the faithful. The ciborium filled with hosts stands on the altar (recall the Offertory when the ciborium is placed there). Consecration during the Holy Mass, distribution of Communion, the preservation of the remaining consecrated hosts for the sick (Drawing of the ciborium with the lid and small veil).

EXPLANATION. We now have this consecrated bread present continually in our church. (Repetition: bread for everlasting life, for uniting us with Christ, for the increase of our grace-life). The Divine Presence! This remains so long as the species of bread is there. Throughout the ages, Christians have paid visits to the church and have venerated the consecrated bread: genuflection, private adoration, sanctuary lamp (on guard: an indication to the faithful).

A particular form of adoration, however, is Benediction. Exposition in the monstrance (Drawing); corporate prayer of the congregation in the presence of Christ hidden in the Sacrament; the

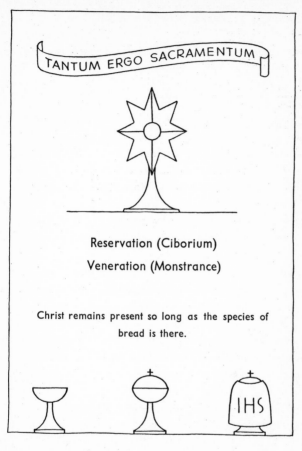

TANTUM ERGO SACRAMENTUM

Reservation (Ciborium)

Veneration (Monstrance)

Christ remains present so long as the species of
bread is there.

blessing (Christ blesses us); hymns of adoration; the "Most Holy
Sacrament of the altar".

APPLICATION. Practice the hymn, "Pange Lingua", "Tantum
ergo", with the Divine Praises and prayer.

80. TEMPTATION

AIM. A sober view of the reality of life with its daily falls plotted by Satan.

PREPARATION. Temptation, sin, punishment (e.g., Adam and Eve, Cain; from the life of the children themselves). In the temptation of Jesus is seen he who stands behind every temptation: the devil.

PRESENTATION. From the epistle of St. Peter: "Be sober, be watchful! For your adversary the devil, as a roaring lion, goes about seeking someone to devour." (1 Peter 5:8).

EXPLANATION. It is the same for everyone, in every occupation, whether young or old, in every age – even in the Church! Ought we to be alarmed at this? Yes, we certainly ought to be, for so many are blind and deceive themselves. They take no account of the enemy, and that pleases him. His aim is to snatch us out of the state of grace so that we lose the grace-life. Deceitful as a serpent, he tries to bring about the fall of everyone. (Drawing.)

But we ought not to be over anxious about him. For we have weapons against him: our free will, prayer, the sign of the cross, the ejaculation, the help of our guardian angel. Here is the good fight: and it is fought all over the world. (Drawing: the serpent pierced by a sword.)

Some carry on this fight winning victory after victory until the end of their life. To them are applied the words of the epistle of the Mass for Confessors (Os justi): "Blessed is the man that is found without blemish . . . he that could have transgressed, and has not transgressed: and could do evil things and has not done them." It is a great thing for anyone to have that said about him.

APPLICATION. Who is the stronger, the one who says "No" to the

Temptation

Be sober, be watchful! For your adversary the devil, as a roaring lion, goes about seeking someone to devour.   1 Peter 5:8

Blessed is the man that is found without blemish.

He that could have transgressed -
and has not transgressed;
could do evil things -
and has not done them!

devil or the one who says "No" to God? Try to prove your answer with an example.

81. MORTAL SIN

AIM. A clear portrayal of mortal sin and its consequences.

PREPARATION. It is not a sin to be tempted. At such a time one often asks oneself: shall I or shall I not? What makes the decision? The Will! That is the faculty with which I make my choice. And that means: I commit sin quite freely. What follows from this fact?

PRESENTATION. The gospel story of the heavenly marriage feast where the king finds a guest who is not wearing a wedding garment. "Friend, how did you come in here? Cast him forth into the darkness outside, where there will be the weeping, and the gnashing of teeth."

EXPLANATION. By the wedding garment is meant the grace-life. This guest had lost it through sin. What is his punishment? Exclusion from the wedding feast = exclusion from heaven, from the Kingdom of God = eternal punishment in Hell. That is the greatest misfortune ever for anyone. For a punishment so terrible one must have done something terrible; something that is called a mortal sin. It makes a line of separation between God and us. (Drawing.)

For a sin to be mortal there are three conditions: grave matter, sufficient reflection, full consent. When all three are present, then the sin is a mortal sin. When one condition is not present or is not quite clear then it is not a mortal sin, but a venial sin.

APPLICATION. Name some sins which are committed: from surprise, from human weakness, after full consideration, through bad habits; and examine each one to see if the three above-mentioned conditions are present.

DISCUSSION. A non-Catholic says that God is too merciful

Mortal Sin

Cast him forth into the darkness outside,
where there will be the weeping, and the
gnashing of teeth.   Matt. 25:30

_____

1. Grave matter
2. Sufficient reflection
3. Full consent

to condemn a man to hell for all eternity. What do you say to
this?

82. VENIAL SIN

AIM. Cause of venial sin and its dangerous effects.

PREPARATION. Some boys find a bottle of poison. The label bears the emblem for poison: a skull and cross bones (Drawing). This means: "Danger of death!" The boys start daring each other. "Who has the courage to drink a drop? A drop won't kill anyone." To do so would not be an act of courage but of terrible frivolity. "Poison is poison, however small the dose."

PRESENTATION. This is how Christians behave who think: "I can see that mortal sin is terrible, but to commit a venial sin is not so bad."

EXPLANATION. With mortal sin the wedding garment is lost, with venial sin it is torn. It could be said that although the grace-life is not lost it receives a wound. There follows wound after wound, which makes for weakness (that is, indifference in the Faith), which puts the life of the Christian in danger, and quite often leads to the death of the grace-life, i.e., to a mortal sin. "Poison is poison, however small the dose."

APPLICATION. 1. Suppose a letter came to you from God: "But have this against you, that you have left your first love. Remember therefore whence you have fallen..." (Apoc. 2:4–5).

2. When does God forgive our venial sins? Sorrow and purpose of amendment, prayer, good works, communion, confession.

Venial Sin

Poison is poison, however small the dose.

You have left your first love
Apoc. 2:4

Forgiveness through: Sorrow and amendment -
good works - communion - confession

83. THE VIRTUE OF PENANCE

AIM. The stages of sorrow.

PREPARATION. If two different people act in the same way, must we always say that what they have done is the same? For example, missing Mass (on account of illness, through lazy indifference). Two pupils stay away from school (one because of a cold, one through fear of a punishment due to him). We can see that all depends, not on the external act, but on the inner reason, or inner motive.

PRESENTATION AND EXPLANATION. It is exactly the same in the three case of sorrow for sin and in asking for forgiveness. There are motives which stand above each other on a mounting stairway.

1. A very troublesome youth had tears in his eyes as he stood before the judge on trial for theft. He was only sorry about the prison sentence the judge would give him. What is the motive for his sorrow? Fear before men. It is called "worldly sorrow". It does not look towards God but towards the world. It has no value before God.

2. A certain person has stayed away from Mass for years because God and religion mean nothing to him. Now he must have an operation and the doctor says that it may not be a success; he may die. He must prepare himself in case the worst happens. He remembers his neglect and goes to confession. He is sorry for his sins because he is frightened by the punishment God could give him. His motive is the "Fear of God". This sorrow is valid, but not perfect: it is called imperfect contrition.

3. We have an example of perfect sorrow in the gospels, "And Peter went out and wept bitterly" (Luke 22:62). Every Good Friday this is sung in church. Who knows why Peter wept? He

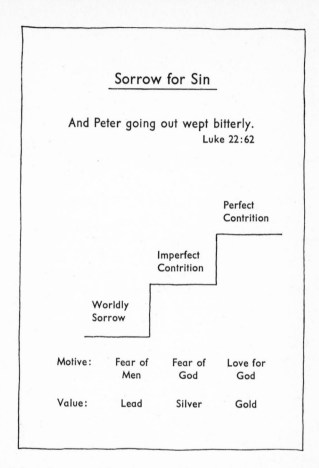

Sorrow for Sin

And Peter going out wept bitterly.
Luke 22:62

	Worldly Sorrow	Imperfect Contrition	Perfect Contrition
Motive:	Fear of Men	Fear of God	Love for God
Value:	Lead	Silver	Gold

had denied Our Lord three times; then the cock crowed, and Jesus being led out by the soldiers looked at Peter, who then realized what he had done. He had betrayed Jesus whom he loved. The thought caused him bitter pain in his heart and he wept bitterly.

97

His motive was "Love of God". This is the highest sorrow; it is called "perfect contrition".

These three kinds of sorrow can be portrayed as on a stairway. One might also compare their value to lead, silver, gold.

APPLICATION. Leo is at the bedside of a dying man: a priest cannot be found. What must he do?

84. THE SACRAMENT OF PENANCE

AIM. The external form of the sacrament as a tribunal, and the institution of the sacrament with the object of meeting the common objection that personal Confession was not taught by Christ.

PREPARATION. There are some famous seats: the throne, the judgment seat, the confessional seat. Whoever sits in these must show something of God: the power, the justice, the grace.

PRESENTATION. A trial scene: a sinner stands before the judge, the prosecutor accuses him. A defence lawyer is also there. The judge examines his guilt and makes a judgment. (This scene can be either narrated or played impromptu after the situation has been outlined: it is particularly important to emphasize the judge's examination of guilt and his judgment and punishment).

EXPLANATION. 1. By means of questions make clear the idea of confession as a trial scene. Who is the accused at confession? "The sinner." Who is the prosecutor? "The sinner also." Who is the judge? "The priest." What has he to do to arrive at a fair judgment? "Hear the accusation and examine it." How does he examine? "By means of questions when something is not clear to him." What happens at the giving of absolution? Here the teacher takes a sheet of paper on which the judge in the play before has written his judgment: very slowly he tears it up before the class

The Tribunal of Confession

Whose sins you shall forgive, they are forgiven them; and whose sins you shall retain,
they are retained. John 20:23

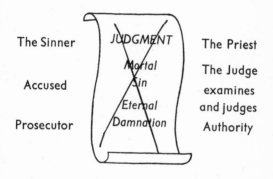

The Sinner	JUDGMENT	The Priest
Accused	Mortal Sin	The Judge examines and judges
Prosecutor	Eternal Damnation	Authority

HOW God forgives he himself decides!

(crossed out in the drawing). This is very impressive and means:
"With the absolution the judgment and the eternal punishment
are torn up. Confession is also a tribunal." This is written up,
and drawn on the blackboard.

2. Where does the priest get his power as a judge from? Christ gave it with the words: "Whose sins you shall forgive ..." (John 20:23). If the priest has to judge whether a sin can be forgiven or not he must first know what the sin is. If therefore someone says: "I confess my sins to God but not to a man. God can forgive me without confession", then we can give him a clear answer: *How* God forgives he himself decides.

APPLICATION. Can the priest give absolution to a sinner in the following cases: When he can return things he has stolen, but will not? when a Catholic confesses that he was married only in a civil ceremony? when someone Confesses he belongs to a society which is against the Catholic Church? when someone goes straight into the confessional without preparing himself, and says that he has prepared already at home;

85. HOW WE SHOULD RECEIVE THE SACRAMENT OF PENANCE

AIM. In the previous instruction we spoke about the actions of the priest in the sacrament of Penance. Now we consider what the sinner has to do.

PREPARATION. The banisters on a staircase make the way safe, particularly for old people, and especially at night. (Drawing: Stairway with five steps and banister.)

At confession also, a banister is necessary: it is invisible in my memory and leads me safely step by step through the sacrament of Penance. The deeper these five steps lie in my memory, the more certain will I be when I go to Confession after school.

PRESENTATION AND EXPLANATION. The five steps are now

What must I do?

1. Examine conscience

2. Sorrow

3. Purpose of Amendment

4. Confession

5. Penance

gone through together and explained with the aid of the Catechism text.

APPLICATION. How often should I go to Confession?

At this age, particularly with boys, difficulties over Confession begin to show themselves. The answer to this question, therefore, ought to suggest various possibilities so that the growing youths will not develop a bad conscience when they depart from the childhood habit of monthly Confession. The following possibilities should be mentioned:

1. Regular monthly Confession. 2. Regular Confession to the same priest. 3. Quarterly Confession. 4. At Easter and Christmas. 5. The minimum to fulfil Church law. 6. Confession after years of absence. In this case especially, the banister makes the return easier.

86. INDULGENCES

AIM. Explanation of Indulgences; the various ways of obtaining them.

PREPARATION. Among men we find both misers and spendthrifts. Ought the Church, with her treasures of grace, to be miserly or generous?

PRESENTATION. Pilgrimage to Rome during the Holy Year. The Holy Door of St. Peter's (Drawing), the Jubilee Indulgence. The joy of the pilgrims over the gift of grace given to them by the Church.

EXPLANATION. The word "indulgence" here means reduction or taking away. What is taken away is some or all of the *temporal* punishment due to sin (sin and eternal punishment are taken away by confession). This difference must be very clearly made and formulated. The inner disposition for gaining an indulgence: prepare oneself for receiving a present. The power to grant indulgences was given by Christ to the Church when he said: "Whatever you bind upon earth shall be bound also in heaven"

102

Indulgences

Sin	temporal
eternal punishment	punishment
Confession	Indulgence

Remission of temporal punishment for sins
which have already been forgiven.

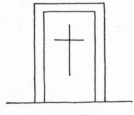

The Holy Door

Plenary Indulgence:
Jubilee Indulgence, Portiuncula, Hour of death

Partial Indulgence:
"Soul of Christ sanctify me . . ."   7 years.

(Matt. 18:18). And the Church, like a generous Mother, dispenses
the treasures of grace given to her by Christ.

APPLICATION. Different indulgences are now mentioned and discussed. Plenary Indulgence – Jubilee Indulgence – Portiuncula –

indulgence at hour of death. (The conditions for gaining them.) Partial Indulgence: meaning of the words, "Indulgence of 1 year, 100 days". For example, the prayer: "Soul of Christ, sanctify me . . .!" (Indulgence of 7 years).

87. THE SACRAMENT OF HOLY ANOINTING

AIM. The children ought to have a good understanding of how to prepare for the sacrament of Holy Anointing.

PREPARATION. The doctor and his medicines. The various remedies: tablets, injections, massage with oil (it penetrates, strengthens). The Anointing of the Sick is a remedy for both body and soul.

PRESENTATION. The teacher, with the aid of a Rituale (if possible), describes the development of a sick call, from the time when the summons reaches the rectory to the giving of the indulgence for the dying. The individual stages are written down, and a drawing is made of the table prepared for the Blessed Sacrament.

EXPLANATION. The Epistle of St. James the Apostle, "Is any one among you sick ?" (James 5:14–15).

The effect of anointing: strengthening against pain; remission of sins, and of punishment due to sin; strengthening for the last moments of death; lightening of the sickness, sometimes curing it.

APPLICATION. Who is right? Gerard says: "It is our duty to tell those seriously ill if they are going to die." Joseph replies that that is cruel. If you were a doctor, would you tell someone seriously ill that he was getting better in order to quieten him? Is that family acting correctly which sends for the doctor again to make sure that their sick son really *is* dying before sending for the priest?

The Anointing of the Sick

1. The priest is sent for
2. The table for the Blessed Sacrament

White cloth - crucifix - candles - flowers - holy
water - cotton-wool - salt - hand-towel

3. Confession
4. Anointing of the sick
   (Eyes - ears - nose - mouth - hands)
5. Holy Communion
6. Indulgence at the hour of death

"Through this holy anointing and his gracious
mercy may the Lord forgive thee what thou hast
sinned through seeing . . . . Amen."

88. THE ORDINATION OF PRIESTS

AIM. The effect of Ordination can be seen in the tasks the priest has to perform.

PREPARATION. At different times in our life we come into contact with various professions; with some for a short while only, with others for the whole of our life. For example, with a teacher (during our school years), with a doctor (in sickness). With the priest? All our life long!

PRESENTATION. When do I come into contact with the priest? All the possibilities are now discussed and drawn up. Baptism (water and the Holy Spirit), in church (façade of the church), religious instruction (note book), Confession (purple cross), Holy Mass (chalice), Confirmation (mitre), youth club (banner or club house), conversation (two chairs and a table), marriage (wedding rings), sick call (bed), Last Sacraments (purple cross), burial (grave or coffin), requiem Mass (covered chalice).

EXPLANATION. If the priest is able to do all that, he must have received a "gift of grace" bestowing on him power and authority. ". . . the grace of God which is in thee by the laying on of my hands." (2 Tim. 1:6). Briefly describe the act of Ordination and also briefly point out the unbroken chain from Christ through the apostles to the bishops.

APPLICATION. 1. Description of a visit to the rectory. 2. Compare a priest and a doctor. 3. How many duties can one find in the vocation of a priest? (Father of a family, administrator of a house, treasurer, teacher, speaker, writer, organizer, liturgist, musician, etc.)

The Priest

in my life

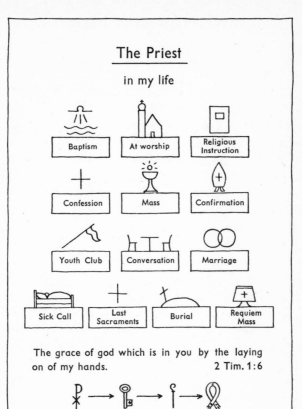

The grace of god which is in you by the laying on of my hands.   2 Tim. 1:6

Ordination of a priest

89. THE SACRAMENT OF MARRIAGE

AIM. An attractive portrayal of Catholic marriage with emphasis on its indissolubility.

PREPARATION. Who has ever closely examined his parents' wedding rings? What do they signify?

PRESENTATION. The teacher describes the religious preparations for the wedding day and the ceremony in the church. The individual stages are written on the blackboard and their importance for the Christian life explained.

EXPLANATION. How do you think the bridal pair feel during the ceremony before the altar? Cheerful – joyful – one of the happiest days of their lives – full of happiness – but also serious? The most serious thing is that here something begins which does not cease until death: through the sacrament the marriage contract becomes absolutely indissoluble. Bride and bridegroom now live together as husband and wife for their whole life. At the beginning it is easy and wonderful: but, as you may know, it can also be very difficult. Sometimes people think that they cannot put up with it any longer and they separate. They decide to part. That is something terrible! For this reason marriage in church is taken so seriously. (Drawing: golden wedding rings with red cross of blessing above. A ring has no end – marriage also!)

APPLICATION. Discussion: What should a young woman do when she finds out that the man she wishes to marry is divorced? Is it right for a man to turn Catholic merely to be able to marry a Catholic girl? Difference between a civil marriage (a contract, which can be dissolved; forbidden to Catholics) and the sacrament of Marriage (a sanctified union and contract before God; indissoluble).

The Sacrament of Marriage

1. Engagement

2. Instruction in Rectory

3. Confession

4. Marriage

5. Nuptial Mass und Communion

What God has joined together let no man
put asunder.   Matt. 19:6

90. VOWS OF RELIGION

AIM. Portrayal of the religious life; its personal worth and its importance for the Church.

PREPARATION. Do you know of any religious houses or monasteries? Why do men and women join religious orders? What do they wear? What do they do?

PRESENTATION. A visit to a Benedictine monastery. Draw the outline of a monastery with the church as the focal point. Every teacher ought to be able to give an insight into life in a monastery from his own experience.

EXPLANATION. A religious binds himself quite freely by vows: to possess nothing, to celibacy, to obedience. These three are called the Evangelical Counsels given by the Church for Christian life. (Point out the gospel foundation: the rich young man; those who remain unmarried for the Kingdom of Heaven's sake). One is free to follow such a counsel or not. First one must examine oneself to make sure that such a counsel is suitable. Entry into a religious order is just as hard as it is wonderful. In a religious order one is *free from* worldly cares and duties (earning one's own living, care for a family), but also *free for* God. (Church services, worship, praying the divine office, reparation, penance) and for work for the Church (teaching, caring for the sick, the Missions).

APPLICATION. Examine the following. Can a young man enter an order: because he is afraid of earning his own living? – because he will then have more time for God than would be possible in the world? – because he wants to serve on the Missions? – because he would like to live a community life in the monastery? – because he wants to get away from home? – because he likes nursing the sick?– because he wants to do something for God? – because he fears the

In a Monastery

The Evangelical Counsels

1. Poverty

2. Celibacy

3. Obedience

Free for God
and to work for the Church

sin in the world and would be safer in the monastery? Plan a lesson with filmstrips on life in a monastery.